Abandoned By All Things

poems by
Karl Koweski

Roadside Press

copyright

Editor: Michele McDannold

Roadside Press
Colchester, Illinois

Table of Contents

For Arthur Koweski,
who supported my shenanigans
with an iron fist.

smuggling sweat socks

I was eleven years old
the day I decided
I might be a little
too short in the pants
to interest the ladies.

I remember looking down
at the front of my
stone-washed jeans
and thinking
there needs to be
a much bigger bulge
happening there.

with my mother
shouting at me to quit
posing before the mirror
and get ready to go,
I grabbed a pair
of balled up
sweat socks and shoved
them down my pants.

I entered that
goddam mall like the
patron saint of porno stars.
never had an eleven
year-old walked
with such swagger,
such big dick confidence.

I did not have
a cent in my pocket
or a hope
to my dreams,
but I had this
oddly spherical
bulge in my pants
enabling my groin
to enter KB Toys
three seconds
before the rest of me.

I tipped a wink
and snap/pointed
at the counter girl
who regarded me
with befuddlement
tinged with what
I could only hope to be
sexual curiosity.

surveying the action figures,
I readjusted the bulge
every three seconds
until it shifted
too far to the left
and the sweat socks
began the slow descent
down my pant's leg.

"can I help you?"
the clerk asked,
more suspicious than
sexually curious
as though she
intuitively grasped
that not only was I
a penile fraud,
but a lowly
sneak thief as well.

"model cars," I mumbled
"where are they?"

"next aisle over."

she stood there
waiting for me
to make my move,
her eyes flickering
to the impressive bulge
at my thigh.

I knew taking a step
would only increase
the sock's rate of descent
but I saw no other
alternative.

by the time I
maneuvered around

the clerk, my knee was
twice its normal size.

something about my
sweaty, furtive demeanor
prompted the clerk
to follow me to
the rack of Testor paint
at which point
my ankle had swollen.

she couldn't take
her eyes off me
and I couldn't take
my eyes off the models
as the balled up
socks popped out
of my pant's leg.
I subtly kicked
the incriminating
evidence away.
the socks rolled
toward the clerk's feet.

"excuse me," she said
"you dropped your socks."

"those ain't my socks,
I'm wearing mine."
I lifted a pant's leg
revealing nearly

identical socks.
"those socks were there
before I got here,"
I added as I
retreated from the store
into the mall proper.

swagger gone forever,
convinced the clerk
somehow, even now,
was alerting
the rest of womandom
to my secret shame.

postscript to smuggling sweat socks

I had a complicated childhood.
I realized pretty early on
I was going to have to struggle
just to qualify as
unconventionally handsome.
it seemed I didn't start
growing hair until I was eight
and I started losing it at nine.
follicly peaking in the third grade
provided a unique challenge
for the remainder of my existence.

I can remember when fellas
perming waves into their bangs
was fashionably acceptable
and I convinced my mother
to carry me to her beautician
so I could get some bounce
seared into my mousy brown hair.
I could see the pity peer from
the hair stylist's green eyes
when she said "oh, honey,
your hair is much too thin for me
to be able to do anything with."
I was twelve years old.

most memories consist of
humiliating snapshots of
trying to surf the tides of

social acceptability,
from ripped jeans and a
gorgeous, stringy mullet
during my Def Leppard era
to dyed black hair and
a blacked-out wardrobe once
I discovered Nine Inch Nails.

when the Doors movie premiered
back in '92 I purchased
a pair of leather pants
and a concho belt from the mall
along with a pair of cowboy boots.
I wore that ensemble every
day for three months straight
until I tired of strangers
continually asking if I were gay.
I retired my leathers the day
a random passerby asked how many
cows did it take to make my costume
and I answered "just one, your mom."
being chased in ninety degree heat
bare-chested, in leather pants and boots,
love bead necklace whipping my face
did not cry out "I am the lizard king".
so did I smuggle sweat socks into
a toy store when I was eleven years old?
you would make a fool out of us both
if you assume anything I write is true.
also, yes, I absolutely did shove socks
down my pants to impress the ladies

at the age of eleven after seeing a
John Belushi skit on SNL.
when I read this poem in public
I can see eyelines shift groin ward
as if forty years later I'd still
be playing the same games
of my water-headed youth.
let me assure you diabetic socks
do little to expand the crotch area
regardless how many pairs
you jam down there.

the raw dogs of reality boulevard

my son leaves for his job interview,
a gig delivering pizzas, resigned more
than excited, bristling at the collared
shirt utterly denuded of Iron Maiden
graphics, hair tucked beneath a ball cap.

upon his return I ask how the interview
went. he shakes out his long hair, sighs.
it didn't work out, he regrets to
inform me, it seems they foolishly
expected him to work nights, delivering
pizza, this boy of mine who refuses
to eat pizzas or hamburgers or
vegetables or anything that doesn't
consist of chicken nuggets and fries.

when the fuck did you expect to deliver
pizzas? Exasperation escalates my volume.

mornings, he replies without a hint
of sarcasm, and I demand to know
who orders pizzas in the morning.
name one goddam place that opens
for business before eleven am.
well, he hedges, early afternoons, I mean.
oh, early afternoons as in your mornings.
so, you can't work reality mornings
and you can't work nights because it
interferes with your storming the forts

and massacring the player characters.
you're basically relegated to a two
hour golden window between the hours
of 1 pm and 3 pm for availability.

he concedes this is true with a shrug
of the shoulders, what can you do?
the gulf stream is on the verge of collapse,
the economy teeters on a razor's edge,
government is gridlocked with a
childishly ideological dysfunction.
no amount of pizzas delivered will
put enough cheddar in his pocket
to afford to live in anything other
than a tar paper shack so why not
let him give up for the both of us?

hard time

a block away from the house
I came of age in,
the Carmelite Home for Boys
dominated half a city block.
a seven-foot-high brick wall
surrounded the sandstone complex,
the entire edifice
radiating hopelessness.

I thought it was a
prison for bad kids
rather than a home
for boys whose parents
could no longer
provide care for them.

so, when my mother
threatened to send me
there, I thought she had
gotten wise to my
petty criminality
rather than simply
tiring of my company
and looking to
abandon me the most
convenient way possible.
constantly curious of
the Carmelite mysteries,
I would climb the roof

of a neighboring garage
during my ninja
escapades and spy
on the children
imprisoned by circumstance
consorting on the
concrete playground.
the metal equipment
resembled a military
obstacle course rather
than the wood and
composite materials
comprising the apparatus
at the playgrounds
I was free to attend.

I watched the children,
watched how they interacted,
looked for weaknesses
and considered how I might
exploit these weaknesses.

and finally I returned home
and apologized to my mom
for all my twisted transgressions
begging her to keep me
a little while longer.

pedaling rainbows

the bicycle was a birthday gift
from my grandparents,
nazi sympathizers, the both of them
eager to carry on Hitler's dream
of eugenics by presenting me
the one bicycle sure to get me
beaten to death before Christmas.

every color of the rainbow
was represented on the
frame of that fucking bicycle.

(this being back before the gays
stole the rainbow from Jesus
though we all suspected even
then, rainbows were kinda fruity)

it was a vibrant array of colors,
canary yellow oranged
into a bloodlust red,
purpling into frost bite blue
greening back to yellow.

tassels fluttered from the
handlebars and I was afraid
to break contact with the
banana seat for fear someone
might notice the graphic of
a cowboy twirling a lasso

while riding a bucking bronco
across an arcing rainbow.

the neighborhood kids
called me "Tootles"
and given the bicycle's lack
of adequate acceleration,
they had no problem
running me down to deliver
one of the frequent beatings
that defined my summer.

two years, I rode that damn bike
which I inexplicably named "Bruce"
until I was able to hand it
down to my younger brother
relishing the future catcalls
and beat downs the bicycle
was sure to usher into his life.

day one, he painted it black.

there is no money in coloring for the flipper-armed masses

I learned the correlation
between art and commerce
at the age of seven years
when, having crayoned
through an entire Black Hole
movie tie-in coloring book
I showed my work to Dad
for his artistic critique.

a day later, he gave
a dollar to me, saying
he sold the coloring book
to a lady at his job site.

even so young, my father's
words struck me as implausible.
why would anyone want
to buy a coloring book that
had already been colored?

my father furrowed his brow,
said something about the
woman's son having been born
with flippers for arms
unable to color his own.
the explanation was
good enough for me.

I rifled through my room

gathering all my old coloring
books and during a hand
cramping Crayola marathon,
managed to fill every
blank page within.

I presented the eight book trove
to my father the next evening
estimating enough capital
represented by that artwork
to purchase three Star Wars figures.

he returned home from work
empty-handed, citing
market saturation and
an increase in supply
versus a decrease in demand,
there being only so many mothers
raising flipper-armed children.

but I figured he just
took the money he earned
from my artistic endeavors
and spent it on booze,
and I vowed from that moment
on, never again to use an
intermediary to sell any
of my masterpieces, again.

abandoned by all things

my brother phones
late at night,
he's been drinking again,
asking if I might write
a few poetic lines
in honor of
our dead father
so Richie G can
temporarily immortalize
the words on
his forearm below
the half-finished angel,
a tribute to a dad
he vaguely remembers
from his early youth.

I haven't written
anything
in nearly a year.
not sure I want
to start now
with this.

brother,
no angel of the
heavenly variety
ever gazed favorably
upon the actions
of our father.

his prayers
never extended beyond
the patron saint of
fast women
and slow horses.

thirty years dead, now,
he lorded over nothing
more regal than
a push broom
and mop bucket.

his navy blue shadow
and watchmen cap halo
have receded into
a dull oblivion
of purposefully
forgotten memories.

I have nothing
more to offer
as eulogy.
he lived and died
as we live and die,
abandoned by all things.

goose steppin' gramma

gramma
left a ruined Germany,
pregnant and married
to a bullet-crippled G.I.
believing
in her heart of hearts
Hitler
was a good man.

one
only had to look
at what he'd done
for the country
before
the allied decimation
of her
homeland.

Hitler
took the people from
the breadline
to the
assembly line
providing
an identity,
a sense of
national pride
absent
for far too long.

gramma
tells me this
when
we are alone,
her parlor reeking of
peppermint schnapps.

it is my
resemblance
to her younger brother,
Paul,
thirteen years old
when he was
captured by the Russians
during the last days
of the war
that breaks her heart

which
doesn't keep her from
dragging her fistful
of diamond-encrusted rings
across my head
when my attention
lags.

you're too weak
to amount
to anything,
she tells me.

you need to
toughen up.

stop reading
so many books.

cancer

amid rumors
of
pestilence

his temple
ruins rise

on the
outcropping
of couch

overlooking
television
vistas.

days
wither
hopes
perish

seasons
end.

I was a fifth grade Jack Ketchum

my desire to write, sadly,
coincides with my desire
to be adulated as a writer.
I can trace this symbiosis
back to the fifth grade where
I scored my first fiction success
with my short story
An Invitation to Death.

the plot, near as I can recall,
involved an invitation extended
to my cousin and I to
investigate a house of
dubious reputation.
within minutes, entering the house
my cousin was devoured by
a slavering shadow monster
while I escaped out a back window.

my classmates hung on every word,
clung to every dangling participle,
reacted with awe and reverence
to the graphic description of
disembowelment, fawning upon me
the sort of literary kudos
I can only dream of recapturing today.
flushed with the respect of my peers
I launched a bevy of sequels.
Invitation to Death II, III, IV…

within which friends and relatives
met all manner of gruesome demises.

by the time I finished penning
Invitation X The Final Invite,
I sensed my literary star descending
losing my status as literary lion
to Leticia who wrote convincingly
of magical ponies in faraway suburbs.

it was too much success too early,
thinking back on all those years since,
toiling away in crushing obscurity.

I never did explain why
the narrator kept returning
to the slaughterhouse, acting
surprised by each gory climax.

under threat of the square and compass

my grown son is shaken to the core,
demanding to know what the Free Masons
are planning to do with all his
personal information they've compiled.

ordinarily, when he rants against
the secret societies, the cartels of
lunatics and capitalistic anarchists,
I chalk it up to paranoia, his
brain is an upset tummy of
half-digested internet news reports
and Tik Tok conspiracy videos.

but, this go around, it seems while
he was searching through a shoe box
of old photographs and keepsakes,
he found a yellowed envelope
stamped with the Free Mason's sigil.

inside, he was horrified to discover
a dossier listing the pertinent
facts of his existence, fingerprints,
a picture of him at seven years old
when he still believed in the moon landing.

at a glance, it was obviously a
service sponsored by the Free Masons
to create info packets for parents
to provide police in the improbable

but never impossible event
a child goes missing, is abducted.

for my son, it is easier to accept
he found his way onto the Free Mason's
radar back in the second grade;
that, even now, they are monitoring
his behavior and activities
hoping to ascertain whether he is
an ally or enemy by
examining his video game skills
and studying his Dungeons and Dragons
problem solving abilities.

the cat's in the cradle, the kid's in the kitty litter

there is a single wide trailer
slouched on a spit of land
like a discarded beer can.
flags festoon junked cars
TRUMP 2024, LET'S GO BRANDON
all these banners of a defeated army
snapping in the Alabama breeze,
rusted appliances and broken toys
appear like crusted lesions in the
leprous, weed-choked yard.

twice a day, to and from the factory,
I pass this eye sore homestead
wondering at the humanity at play
behind the coke can, press wood walls.
the last week of March, the couple,
Logan and Charla, injected some
bad dope leaving behind their
two-year-old son and
six-month-old daughter
with a DVD of Paw Patrol
for company and dry cat food
and a bowl of water for sustenance.

five days passed before concerned
relatives checked in, finding two
decomposing corpses in the bedroom
and two malnourished children
wallowing in their own filth.

usually, when I relate this story
I'll try to add a little levity.

the cat's in the cradle,
the kid's in the kitty litter,
shit like that
mining that rich vein of clever
humor running through my core.

but the jokes
are only tiny absurdities
meant to obscure
the horrible truth.

the end of the galaxie

my eyes, my mind barely registers
the oil-stained rectangle of dirt.
it is only when I notice the
intake manifold strewn in the grass
I realize my front yard is minus
one 1974 Ford Galaxie LTD.

stolen, I think… no, impossible,
not with four flat tires, dead battery,
ruptured radiator, punctured carburetor,
wasp nests colonized throughout.
the car hadn't moved in five years.

my grandfather bought the car new
the year I was born, drove it locally,
mostly to church and work, and when
I inherited the car thirty years later,
I drove it everywhere except church and work.

the Ford delivered me from the narrow
side streets of Chicago's east side
to the gravel country roads of Alabama
where the LTD's chicken shit brown
paint scheme complimented the
scent of chicken shit fertilizing
the fields surrounding my house trailer.
the Galaxie remained mobile another decade
before the onslaught of years and the
explosion of gasoline prices conspired to

transform the hulk into a lawn ornament,
a monument to my mechanical incompetence.
yet, I held out hope I could some day
earn enough money to hire a professional
capable of replacing the brake lines,
rebuild the engine, bomb the wasp nests,
and figure out a way to get the
whole thing to run on electricity.

all gone, almost a half century sold out
from under me, this iron brother from
the geographical womb, two tons
of Detroit steel, replaced by
four crisp twenty dollar bills,
the scrapyard equivalent of
thirty pieces of silver presented to me
by my Judas wife who'd been
threatening this betrayal since the first
opossum took up residence beneath the hood.

and I wonder how much time remains
to me, how soon before I'm harvested
for spare parts with nothing to show
for the duration of my existence
but a rectangular patch of dirt.

dungeons and dragons and me

I still wake up from dreams
where I'm rolling five
six-sided dice
picking the three highest rolls.

strength
intelligence
wisdom
dexterity
constitution
charisma

a character page
teeming with attributes,
proficiencies, and equipment,
and a plethora of
polyhedral dice
all conspiring to keep me
from having sex.

it is no coincidence
rolling dice and jerking off
require the same wrist motion.

I'm still haunted by the
nonchalant way I'd slip my
Player's Handbook from my
school bag during study hall
oblivious to the pretty girls
rolling their eyes at me.

strength
intelligence
wisdom
dexterity
constitution
charisma

always the lowest dice roll
placed in charisma,
unaware of the importance
of human interaction.

always the highest dice roll
placed in strength
because I possessed none.

life being so simple
when it's parsed down
to numbers and
levels of experience.

it's all just a roll of the dice

my daughter breezed through school,
graduated effortlessly near the top of her class,
found her calling in speech language pathology,
earned her master's degree and immediately
found a job she enjoys making a difference
in children's lives, while she's bringing home
enough money to buy a house, a new
vehicle and take exotic trips often.
I'm proud of her accomplishments,
humbled by her decency, her humanity.
she is beautiful inside and out.
she radiates an aura of love and peace.
and none of this had anything to do with me.
she carried herself with poise and the
determination to succeed on her own lofty terms
from the moment she climbed out of the cradle.

my son once started his evening shift at
the Kentucky Fried Chicken an hour later
than his 5pm start time claiming he overslept.
he skated by through high school unaware of
such things as a GPA, with grand plans of becoming
a welder the same way some folks announce
their goals of becoming a novelist having never
inked the first word onto a sheet of paper.
he spoke often of becoming a history professor
due to his love of military-themed video games.
he could recount most of the major battles from
most of the significant wars, the armaments,

strategies, the countries involved, without ever
having opened a book, and he seemed undaunted
when I explain to him he was not going to be
able to lecture a classroom of university students
by firing up the Xbox, playing Call of Duty.

but he's a good kid, kind-hearted, loves animals,
keeps a small circle of close friends who share
his similar interests. he never asks for much,
would be content in this life with a cot,
a laptop, decent wifi, and chicken tenders.
he eschews drugs and alcohol, avoids women
for fear of comprising his agenda of indifference,
whereas my daughter married her high school sweetheart,
shares a relationship based on love and
understanding and the desire to lift one another
up and support each other unconditionally.

they were both raised in the same household,
but only one of them at an early age was
indoctrinated into the Dungeons and Dragons.

the saint of slaying snakes

the Koweski clan cowering
in the car port were immediately
reminded of Saint George,
his boot heel triumphantly grinding
the satanic dragon's neck as the
hero's spear pierced its dark heart,
by the way I battled the
three-foot-long black snake
coiled atop the screen door.

after an hour-long skirmish,
countless feints with the garden hoe
numerous near miss jabs
with the rusted machete,
several strategic retreats,
I finally managed to dispatch
the serpent with a series
of frenzied blade chops
to its spade-shaped head.

now, it could be argued
this innocent creature
was chased to the high ground
of the patio door by the
latest deluge of thunderstorms
and wished for nothing more
than to live and let live.
and were I trekking through
the woods and happened upon

the slithering son of a bitch,
I would allow it its life.

a black snake showing up
on my doorstep, however,
is committing suicide by
Polack, in my estimation.

anyway, I killed the snake
in spectacular fashion,
and by the time I have
embellished this story by
the hundredth retelling,
future generations of the
Koweski progeny
will be relaying the history
of how Saint Polish Hammer
slaughtered Godzilla
armed with only a buck knife
and a bad attitude.

bird cage safari

the old lion
broken-toothed, boredom beaten
lies in the dust
within a fenced enclosure.
there's twice daily rations
of rancid antelope meat
and the scent of the
Serenghetti on the wind
in mockery of freedom.

five tourists enter
the old lion's confines,
their soft hands more familiar
with golf clubs than firearms.

they prop high-powered
hunting rifles
against pudgy shoulders.
gleeful eyes peer through lenses
so magnified
the fleas worrying the beast's
narrow, mangy flanks
appear large as sparrows.

an investment banker fires first
raising a clot of dirt
near the lion's left front paw.
an architect draws first blood
nicking flesh from its rump.

the rifle's flat crack discharges
echoes over unknown miles.
the old lion is aware of a
distant flapping of wings,
like a fleeting memory
of youth and instinct
and the rush of the hunt.

the old lion's eyes flicker
with a semblance of life,
of heart and hate and heat
and the taste of meat
rent from quivering bone,
the sudden flood of blood gravy
accompanied by a
screaming, bleating orchestra.

the old lion's roar
sends gazelles racing
five miles away.

the tourists yank triggers
with little regard for aim
or frenzied orders shouted
by their great white guide
who organized this
bird cage safari
for five grand a head.

in a streak of wiry muscle

and tawdry mane,
crazed eyes and jagged fangs,
the old lion charges.

bullets zing air, thwack dirt.
gurgling growls underscore
rushed prayers and beseechments
for divine intervention.

as bullets find flesh
the old lion lunges,
one final apex predator leap
for the searing white sun above
and the grave black beetles below,
swiping at the jugular of
a lawyer from Alabama
who can only evacuate
his bowels as the old lion's
claws cleanly bisect the
Kevlar-plated binoculars
hanging around his neck
like a warmonger's crucifix.

momentum carries
the old lion another three yards
before it collapses.
meager, perforated chest shuddering
against the final stillness.

it is only then the COO of
a hydraulic manufacturing

facility steps out from behind
his high school era buddies
and crows "holy shit!
was that a rush or what?"

the ballad of Kevin Greeson

the sons of Kevin Greeson
know their father died
a patriot to the end,
his heart flagging long
before his unwavering
love for Trump and country.
trading his fishing poles
for automatic weapons
he declared on social media
let's take this fucking country back.

to the world at large
Kevin Greeson fell off
a chair inside the capital
building while trying to
remove a portrait from
the wall during the
January 6th insurrection,
and, in doing so,
Kevin Greeson tased himself
in the testicles.
unable to disengage,
the unmerciful electric
jolt coursed through
his balls until his
patriotic heart gave out.
now, some folks on the
conservative side of things
will tell you not the first

volt of juice invaded his
nutsack, that he did not
even reach the interior.
Kevin Greeson simply got
too excited sticking it
to the liberals and given
his high blood pressure,
perhaps a penchant for
greasy cheeseburgers
morning, noon and night,
a heart attack was
only a natural result
of attempting to overturn
a democratic election.

but I would rather embrace
the fake leftist news
imagining Kevin Greeson's
dying moments smelling
his own frying pubic hair
as he did the electric jig
thinking not of his wife
and children, but of that
great man, Trump, and how
he had that election
unfairly stolen by Biden.

anyway, Kevin Greeson's dead
and his family is left
with a shrine of the man,
adorned with pictures of

the martyred patriot
posing with his AR-15s
his MAKE AMERICA
GREAT AGAIN cap
perched atop his urn.
heart and testicles and
his hope for a second term
reduced to ashes much
like his hero's legacy.

the UAW killed my daddy

two days before the scheduled union vote,
the corporate CEO, Dick Whitaker
drove out from the main office in Atlanta
in his convertible BMW, launching
a last-ditch effort to thwart what
we believed would be a UAW victory.

as the third shift crew leaned back
in their folding chairs, eyes lidded,
frowns stone-set, everyone perpetually
tired, ready to just get it over with,
Whitaker stepped before the assembly
and loosened his tie for a third time,
a calculated move, as though by
easing the ligature around his neck
he could gain the confidence of a
room full of machinists who'd had
their wages frozen these last five years,
benefits chipped away to nothing.

for the third time, this third meeting,
Whitaker allowed his eyes to mist
and his voice crack with emotion
when he announced the union killed
his father with the cold certainty
of a .44 bullet through the heart.
his daddy, to hear Whitaker tell it,
was the best damn paint mixer
DuPont Industries had ever employed.

he could match paint with a precision
no computer could possibly duplicate.
when DuPont went union it
nearly broke his daddy's heart,
what with the union's promises
of competitive wages, employee
rights and lucrative benefits,
his daddy knew his days at the
factory were hopelessly numbered.

sure enough, not even ten years later,
DuPont decided they no longer needed
his expertise. however, rather than
cast him aside, the company
dispassionately offered him a position
at another DuPont plant located
clear across the country.

clear across the country, he repeated,
allowing the insult to sink in.
my daddy lived in Iowa his whole life
except for his service in the army.
the thought of leaving the only place
he'd ever known tormented daddy.

here, he turned away from the assembly,
dabbing at his dusty, reptilian eyes.
after a reasonable amount of silence
and two well-timed shoulder
hitches, he faced the machinists.

last time I saw my daddy at Kinnick
stadium where I was a starting
cornerback for the Hawkeyes, I barely
recognized my daddy, so great
the toll the union had taken on him.
his heart gave out on him toward
the end of the game's third quarter.
now, I have no doubt in my mind,
the union was responsible for his death.
after the UAW came into DuPont
my daddy was never the same again.
now, I'm not going to tell you
how to vote; I only ask you to
think of your children and what kind
of effect a union shop will have on them.

the machinists glanced at each other,
mirroring what-the-fuck? expressions.
I finally raised my hand, stood up,
nervously addressing the CEO,
my bosses, my assembled co-workers.

I feel for your loss, Mr. Whitaker.
I, too, lost my father to the unions.
Whitaker tightened his lips, sympathetically,
or maybe to avert a creeping smile.

you see, I continued, my father was
drinking at a local bar when a teamster
mistook my father for the guy who pissed
on the teamster's Camaro and

the fella punched Dad in the face
resulting in a bar clearing brawl.
six years later, my father was dead
from the pancreatic cancer, but I know
with the same certainty you have
it was the UAW what killed my daddy.

you can call me Captain Gringo

Charles, the third shift maintenance man,
brought the books to work
inside two Reebok shoeboxes.

the name of the author
was an obvious pseudonym given the
pornographic nature of the novels.
the twenty-nine volumes were gathered
under the RENEGADE imprint
chronicling the turn-of-the-century
adventures of Captain Gringo
and his lusty French sidekick, Gustave,
who, during their south of the border
campaigns, fucked a vast array of
senioritas, sheep, paraplegics, whores,
prairie dogs, and a guy named Lou.

not to be outdone by the Frenchman,
Captain Gringo with his nine inch tool
also fucked everything that walked
or crawled or galloped and
what he didn't fuck he usually killed
with his twin gatlin guns.
often, he'd be called upon to kill
what three pages earlier
he had thoroughly fucked.
Charles swore these books were
classic literature, and, before long,
we were agreeing with him.

men who hadn't picked up anything
wordier than the Sunday Times
devoured the Captain Gringo shenanigans
at a three book a week clip.

the books were hackneyed, tedious,
poorly written throughout but
I read them compulsively, imagining
myself tearing ass through Mexico
fucking the Generalisimo's twin
daughters, his nymphomaniacal wife,
their coy, elderly housekeeper,
and their bushy-tailed Pomeranian
before rampaging into town
big dick and twin guns blazing.

and when I glanced about the factory,
I noticed my co-workers also
walking the aisles with a bit more swagger
looking for men to challenge, women
to ravage, stray mutts to cornhole,
and, finding none, returning to their
machines and the dog-eared paperbacks
sequestered beneath their work instructions.
a shop floor teeming with Captain Gringos
and not a Gustave among us.

promotion

after twenty years
working on the floor
six, seven day weeks
ten, twelve hour days
slinging metal
chroming hydraulic
cylinders, always
saying yes,
whatever it takes,
to pay the bills
keep food on the table
clothes on our backs,
all the cliches
of a capitalistic
society, I've been
promoted up into
management,
replacing physical
strain with some
mental stress in
order to destroy
me completely.
the absurdity of
becoming a supervisor
is not lost on me.
I have become the
wood-handled axe
entering the forest.
and, though I refuse

to chop down
any trees,
it seems I'm content
just to merely
watch them fall.

the aftermath of getting beaten half to death by three hipsters

as I lay beaten half dead
on the Circle K asphalt next
to a spent wad of Bubbalicious
watching the man bun crested heads
recede atop fixed gear bicycles
I vowed I'd have my revenge.

I just thought it'd take a few months
given my penchant for procrastination.

last night, however, vengeance was mine.
with the band, Dysania (don't bother
looking them up, the band is so obscure
even Google doesn't know who the
fuck they are), performing at the Juggling
Jester microbrewery, I realized
since there were only thirty-five hipsters
within a thousand mile radius aware
of Dysania's existence, there was
a better than decent chance my
assailants would be in attendance.

I arrived incognito, which is to say,
I opted against wearing an Iron Maiden shirt.
I decided to lure them outside the venue
by waylaying their fixed gear bicycles
with my Keith Moreland signed
baseball bat. unfortunately, the attack

occurred in the midst of a blistering
glockenspiel solo, and the ruckus
of jackass transportation getting
demolished went unheeded.

so I chained the doors and set the
building ablaze with gasoline.

fuck those guys.

interestingly enough,
the howls of hipsters burning alive
resembles a cross between
yodeling and Mongolian throat singing.

doing poems on aircraft carriers

Tommy Tuberville,
the mostly evil, largely senseless
senator of Alabama
compiled a record of
85 wins, 40 losses
while the head coach of the
Auburn college football program.

now, anyone south of Kentucky
and east of the Mississippi
will tell you this winning percentage
for this school
is a feat so miraculous
had the majority of Alabamians
favored Catholicism over the
bat shit crazy strain of Christianity,
Tommy Tuberville would
have been canonized as a saint.
as it were, he was nominated
for the next best thing,
public office.

his politics centers on,
in the parlance of our times,
riding Donald Trump's dick.
such an affiliation has led
Tommy Tuberville to say and do
some incredibly stupid fucking things.

his latest mindblower
involves complaining that
"we've got people doing poems
on aircraft carriers
over the loudspeakers."

people who don't do poems
were aghast at this revelation.
what's next? they asked themselves.
drag shows on the flight deck?

people who do do poems
simply shrugged their shoulders
knowing performing for even
a captured audience rarely
equates to book sales,
literary fame, or inspires
the sullen masses to invest
the slightest interest in the arts.

October 16, 2016

God visited me that chilly
mid-October day at a moment
I was so isolated, so lonely,
I'd gone past the casual viewing
of clown porn to a point
where I was nonironically
spinning glam rock albums
which would have shamed me
back when Nirvana was still
some Buddhist bullshit.

upon appearing in my kitchenette,
the snow-bearded deity
all but ignored the Saigon Kick
song blaring from the speakers
and pronounced "I'm giving
you a choice, here, and you can
only pick one or the other.

Cubbies winning the World Series
Trump losing the presidential election…

one or the other
you can not have both."

"Cubbies World Series," I answered
without the slightest hesitation.

how bat shit crazy could Trump

truly be? surely, there were
enough checks and balances in
Washington to keep that goofy
orange bastard from bringing the
country to the brink of a Korean
style nuclear barbecue or
twitter flame wars with the
Australian prime minister…

and this was the Cubbies, here.
my father lived and died,
his father lived and died,
without witnessing the boys in blue
basking in the ultimate glory.

God nodded his head, knowingly
perhaps even nonjudgementally.

does this snap decision
delivered in the grip of
post-season desperation
make me responsible for the
political landscape as
it exists today?

I don't know.
I'd prefer to blame the
seventy million Americans
who can't differentiate
television fantasy from
groin kick reality.

thinking back, maybe it wasn't God
who visited me that late afternoon.
it could have been my neighbor
Sam Halligan who had also
taken to cultivating a magnificent
beard, though his face carpet
was more Duck Dynasty,
less Mount Olympus,
and he was forever asking me
jackassy hypothetical questions
like "would you rather have sex with
Melissa McCarthy or Rebel Wilson?"

doesn't matter.
I made my decision.
now, Anthony Rizzo has a
World Series ring and
the world wobbles on the brink
of a spectacular collapse.

thank you, God.

Ron Santo looks out from heaven into the stinking crater called Wrigley Field where Satan landed after being cast out of paradise

I stood by the Cubbies my entire life
until the diabetes took my legs,
and then I just sat there
in this motherfucking wheelchair
watching the team to whom I devoted
my entire existence, year after year,
chip away at my remaining dignity
as the front office fielded a bunch
of aging, overpaid, unmotivated losers
signing lucrative contracts ensuring
they'd never have to play hard again.
the numerical margin of my tombstone
may read 2010, but let me tell you,
I died way back in 2003, I died
the moment that cocksucker in headphones,
Steve Bartman, reached out and deflected
that goddam baseball from the glove of
that light-hitting, slow-moving, lackadaisical
fielding Moises Alou with five outs
remaining before the Cubbies first trip to
the World Series since before it mattered.
five outs! Moises Alou should have sprouted
wings from his ass, flew up, and caught
that fucking ball. he was paid enough.
he owed the Cub's Legion at least one miracle.
I knew then as well as every Cub's fan
who's ever watched the pennants flap

against the frigid wind blowing in that
Dusty Baker would leave Mark Prior
in the game though his arm was jelly and
the fire in his belly all but extinguished.
Mark Prior would stay in the game
regardless of a bullpen teeming with
fifty million dollars' worth of pitching.
so I wasn't surprised the Cubbies blew the lead,
and wasn't surprised when the Cubs lost
the seventh game of the NCLS.
and don't even get me started on that waste
of a shortstop's life, Alex Gonzalez.

death is never really a surprise, is it?
a shock, sometimes…
a let down
but, dying…
it is as inevitable
as a post season meltdown
in Wrigleyville.

you would figure with heaven,
there'd be Cubs banners flapping
from the gleaming spikes of the pearly gates,
Saint Peter wearing a Cub's cap
saying "welcome home, Ron Santo,
hall-of-fame third baseman and
the voice of Chicago Cub's radio.
come on in and grab a mitt,
and have yourself a game of catch.
the Budweisers are always cold

and the Cubbies never lose."
yeah, but that shit didn't happen.
in heaven, the Cubs games ain't
even televised; Harry Carey's been
ducking me and I still don't
have my motherfucking legs.

I think I caught a glimpse of
Jesus Christ wearing a Yankees jersey.
though, to be fair, my eyesight
ain't what it used to be
with the diabetes and all.
it could have been John Lennon.

when I look out from this great expanse
of social mediocrity that is heaven,
I can see the earth below,
the crater where the brightest angel landed.
the angel who would not serve,
the angel who thought he knew better,
the angel who would not have left
a dead-armed pitcher in the game
with the World Series on the line.
I wish I could have had
just one more day in those bleachers
singing "take me out to the ballgame,"
preferably in late October of 2016.

blue futility

seven hundred miles
south of Wrigley Field
on a baseball diamond
atop the second highest
mountain in Alabama,
my five-year-old son
crouches near the
third base bag.
his glove hovers an
inch above the dirt,
batting gloves jut
out of his back pocket,
a wad of Big League Chew
hyperextends his cheek.
he's ready for anything
as long as it is a
softly rolling ground ball.
he looks like a
little ball player
except for one thing.

"Jared, where's your
Cubbies hat?"

"no!"

"where's your Cub's lid, boy?"

"I hate the Cubbies."

"put on your Cub's hat
or I'm gonna run out
there and jump kick you."

"I like the Cardinals."

we stand diametrically
opposed across a
baseball chasm
wider than the
280 miles between
St. Louis and Chicago,
and if he's better off
breaking the cycle
of heartbreak now
before chronic defeat
gets its hooks into him
I'll never admit it.

a shameful uniformity

I can't quantify my hatred
for the Cub Scouts,
but it is always there,
seething,
just below the surface.

those brightly colored merit badges
and bullshit ribbons,
pseudo survivalist camping trips,
pinewood derby races
rewarding the children
possessing the most industrious fathers.

the cub scouts,
a militaristic outreach program
with the sole aim
of selling Orville Reddenbacher popcorn
to the clueless masses.

so reminiscent of that other
haven for pedophiles,
the Klu Klux Klan
charging $200 to join
another $250 for the fancy robes
then, every year they change the
design of the hem forcing you
to buy new robes if you wish
to remain au currant with your jackass
buddies, only to finally discover

you still have to do a bake sale
and sell rebel flag bumper stickers
just so your klavern can afford
to attend the hate rally
sponsored by the local Chik-Fil-A
down in Pawntatawk, Mississippi.

everything is a racket.

terminal destination

the bus station
is more an outpost
than a terminal.

small and grimy
linoleum like plaque
on decaying teeth.
six molded plastic chairs
huddled like old men
awaiting nursing home death.

it is empty except for
the attendant and I
and a vending machine
harboring inedibles.

outside the plate glass,
the Windmill Motel,
the Industrial Strip,
trucking companies
all of it entwined
with the interstate,
asphalt and concrete,
weed-choked and sprinkled
with broken glass
like blood diamonds.
I slot a dime in
the gumball machine,
get a handful of

stale Chiclets
like chewing teeth.

the lobby's desolation
amazes me.
citizens should be
lined up for miles
awaiting the first bus
out of here.

can I help you?
the attendant asks.
my continued presence
upsets her, disrupts
her reading, a book
she holds low
making it impossible
for me to discern
the title and author.

I recite the bus number
and ask for an ETA,
and she tells me
the bus is not due
until tomorrow evening.
her expression is
as difficult to read
as the cover
to her novel.

she refuses eye contact

when I tell her
my lover is on the bus
and after all this time
I get to see her again.

I glance at the calendar
on the wall behind her,
yellowed paper boasts
the wrong month of
a different year.

outside, I spit the
hardened gum into
the weeds, breathe in
the refinery-scented air,
everywhere the rush
and roar of mobility.

I take the long walk
back to the soup kitchen,
thinking how strange
no matter what
bus number I give
it is never scheduled
to arrive until
tomorrow.

dysania

my inner monologues
are just so much white noise
through which the ghosts of my past
attempt to communicate.

some days I convince myself
the voices have receded,
beaten flat, unrecognizable
by the hammer of factory time.

the penknife of conscience
dulls down to
a shoehorn of indifference
I use to wedge myself
into the tight fit of another day.

sweet release *or*
Wilford Brimley says fuck you

all these years
I never allowed the drugs
to plant their hooks into me.
the pills and the powders,
I could pick them up
and put them down
at will
and I was lucky enough
to do so.

the booze
never got on top of me.
moderation was the key.
rare were the days
I had one too many
or one too few.

the women…
they came the closest
to being the end of me.
one or two
over the years, maybe more.
love seizes me
by the throat and squeezes
until I feign death.
then with enough time
my heart beats again
for my next true love.

in the end
it was sugar
that finally got my ass.
not cocaine, not whiskey,
not tattooed blondes.
it was the gummi bears,
the Swedish fish,
bored eating
fistfuls of skittles
that ushered in my demise.

I have to admit
death by sugar
it certainly appeals
to my absurdist nature.

because I did not die of an overdose at 28

I am so diabetic
I can't even listen to
Def Leppard's magnum opus
"Pour Some Sugar on Me"
while frequenting the titty flop.

I have to request the
deejay play Mr. Big's
obscure rendition of
"Shake a Little Stevia On It."

fingers tapping the beat
on this sweaty glass of water,
all that I'm allowed these days
if I want to keep my feet.

as the heavily tattooed stripper
halitosis whispers
she's looking for a hard nine,
it is difficult for me
to conceal my delight
when I reveal to her that
through diet and exercise
my A1C level
is now under seven.

**that Japanese word for when you have more books
than you could possibly read**

every time I see an estate sale
featuring a collection of books
I think, there goes one more bibliophile
dead before he could complete his library.

every time I look upon my own
thousands and thousands of volumes,
the shelves of signed first editions,
the trove of Arkham House treasures,
very few gaps in my Stephen King hardbacks,
nearly every first print Joe R Lansdale,
most of them signed by the maestro.
Charles Bukowski books before
Ecco engulfed Black Sparrow Press
and all the ones after.
my Clive Barker firsts signed and
doodles of monstrosities on the title page.
Easton Press and Folio Society leather bound.
Paperbacks From Hell in their
demonic covered legion.
Arturo Perez-Reverte's English translated run.
Umberto Eco, Nick Tosches, Paul Theroux,
all of Westlake, Richard Stark, Tucker Coe,
Andrew Vachss, Elmore Leonard by the drove,
Hard Case Crime books by the score.
every book you could ever want.
every book I could ever want,
except a Cormac McCarthy signed

first edition of Blood Meridian
forever out of reach.

the most extensive, privately-owned
personal library in all of
Northern Alabama waiting
to be donated to Goodwill
the day after I die.

small carnival on the edge of a Foodland parking lot

when you look at me
there are
twin white stars
reflected
on your glasses
from the ferris wheel
revolving
at my back.

it's just another
trick of the light.

all the carnies smoking cigarettes
like inmates pacing the yard,
they've seen this all before.

the rocket ships blast up and down,
the carousel cars turn round and round,
spinning circles everywhere you look.

everyone going nowhere fast.

the carny at the game booth
hooks you with the promise
of a prize with every chance.

and of all the chances
that I took,
the price always outweighs the prize,

every single time,
yet I win.
every time I see you smile,
I win.

when you look at me
our eyes behind those
twin white stars,
your eyes hold
all the love and disappointment
in the world.

we never rode the ferris wheel.
I promised we would.
we never rode the ferris wheel
at that small carnival
on the edge
of the Foodland parking lot.

the battle above the clouds

the brochure for
the Battle of Chattanooga
reenactment
presented illustrations
of war-weary men
garbed in Union blues
and Confederate grays
armed with Kentucky
rifles and cannonade.

having paid forty dollars
admission to witness
this reenactment,
my expectations were
immediately challenged
when my family and I
were led into a
midget auditorium.

there were five rows
of seats on risers
situated around a
civil war diorama.
hordes of blue and
gray toy soldiers
were positioned
throughout alongside
a paper mache
Lookout Mountain

looming over the
trainset apocalypse.

my slow burn began
as the house lights dimmed
and a recorded voice
narrated the events
leading up to the
battle of the clouds.

as the voice-over droned
Christmas lights
blinked on and off
in the appropriate areas:
Brown's Ferry,
the west face of
Lookout Mountain,
Missionary Ridge.

yellow lights signified
the syncopated pops
of weapons firing.

my daughter fell asleep
before Grant was
promoted to supreme
commander of the west,
taking charge of
the Union forces
exemplified by the
white bulb on the out

skirts of Chattanooga.

my wife played solitaire
on her phone while
General Hooker
and his men seized
Orchard Knob.

after the reenactment
climaxed to a
crescendo of blinking
lights and muffled canon
blasts and canned screams
of dying militia men
from the subwoofers,
we were ushered into the
gift shop by a clerk
who refused eye contact.

in the gift shop
I dropped another fifty
dollars to buy my son
a Union cap and a
plastic long rifle.

"who's the blue guys?"
I quizzed my son.

"the good guys!
the Americans!"
the boy answered.

"and the gray guys?"

"they're the bad guys!
the Nazis!"

I patted his shoulder.

he'll do just fine
in the Alabama
public school system.

red star descending

I've never been good with affairs,
I've never been able to
compartmentalize my emotions.
despite what I say to the contrary,
I fall in love easy,
fall out hard.

I'm addicted to the heart sick
enchantment,
excitement and disillusionment,
the hope and crippled expectations
that comes with giving oneself
over unconditionally
to someone
with a list of conditions.

but don't read this as a warning
or as an invitation
to scorch your flesh
on the heat
of my white hot obsession.
I'm incapable of burning
anyone other than myself.

beware instead
of the black hole left in my wake,
the implosion of passions
as our shared time and space collapses,
leaving an absence so total

not even memory
can escape its allure.

pink star descending

taped to the pink wall
of my adolescent daughter's
room is a hand drawn poster
hyping her imaginary band,
Polly and the Petal Pushers,
spackled with brightly
colored flowers and a
playlist of songs she wrote.

titles like "Lonely Unicorn,"
"I Love Him But He Don't Know I Exist,"
"Smencils, Smencils, Smencils,"
and a cover of the classic
"Don't Bogart That Joint."

seeing her rock star fantasy
I'm transported back,
memories of my own bedroom
and the names of bands
never formed magic-markered
on my closet wall
like a Christmas wishlist.

"Clown Shit Candy,"
"Zitface Paranoia,"
"Dead Puppies For Stangled Children."
the only difference being
my daughter possesses
talent, enough

natural ability
to justify the
sacrifices made
for guitar lessons
and voice coaching.

for me a case of
utter tone deafness
proved to be an
unconquerable foil.

I owned a guitar
since I was twelve,
a Sears catalogue
Stratocaster knock-off,
a six-string sign
from God I was meant
to rock the world,
only to embrace atheism
a week later when
I couldn't master
the opening chords to
Stairway to Heaven.

I've only ever been
a bad impersonation
of my fantasies.

my daughter, though,
she has a chance
to realize her dreams

and that saddens me
more than anything
knowing she will
eventually settle
for so much less.

I should have read the biography

I've been wooing her
with direct messages to
her social media account
for several months now,
and I think
I'm finally getting somewhere.

I adore her poetry.
I appreciate her mind.
her tall, lithe figure,
wildly tousled black hair
and strategically placed
tattoos are of some interest.

I tell her she reminds me
of Anais Nin with her
fearless, confessional style,
writing bursting with
a pagan exuberance.

which is to say, I might
like to remind her of
Henry Miller with his raging
libido in a literary context
and aversion to labor.
I could see myself
being the Henry Miller
to her Anais Nin.

Anais Nin, huh…
she mulls this over.
you know, Anais Nin
seduced her father while
she was in her thirties,
and, at one point, had
an abortion during
her third trimester.

I consider this
new information
and quickly pivot,
offering to be
the Ted Hughes to
her Sylvia Plath.

excommunication

you are the altar
I sacrifice myself upon,
the gateway to divinity.

you are the one of no cloth,
the self-perpetuating myth,
the godhead of fractured faith
anointing the flesh of the
devout with holy secretions.

you are a miracle of seduction,
a transubstantiation
of flesh to obsession,
blood to eternal passion.

I would walk on water for you,
the water would taste like wine
as it touches your lips.

you created the world I live,
set forth the commandments
I abide by.
you instilled the conception
of heaven I strive for.
you issued glimpses of eden
I seek to return to and warned
against the hell of your absence.

I adore you.

I worship you.
I love you before all others,
a love like the universe,
infinite yet expanding.
I have become
the reflection of your image
mirrored in the
cosmic eye of eternity.

on hands and knees
I pray you will not
forsake me when
circumstances conspire
to crucify me
upon the crosses
of inconvenience,
indifference.
the crucifixions
steadily approaching
a horizon of horrors
promising everlasting strife.

the monster wears a husband's face

I've become the
marital equivalent
of a serial killer
defined by the
secrets I conceal,
the casual cruelty
with which I engage
all aspects of life.

my wife only knows me
by the chosen masks
designed only to reveal
whichever emotions
she wishes to recognize.
but even my masks
all wear disguises.

my eyes are mirrors
reflecting light,
creating an illusion
of infinite depth
where only surface exists.

with my moral compass
shattered, my desires
become the stars by
which I navigate a
sea of false alibis.

my cock is the blade
I wield to murder
my wife's dreams,
mutilate her hopes,
and disembowel her
happily ever afters.

I carve her heart out
over and over again,
this trophy I'm compelled
to claim continually.

and when I'm discovered,
as I realize
I someday must,
I will leave behind
a confusing case file
stocked with interviews
of oblivious friends
and relatives
who only remember
a quiet, decent
young, family man
who wouldn't
hurt a fly.

stick figure family

we are only a family
in the stick
figure portraits
my six-year-old
crayons in the margins
of his Red Robin
children's menu.

four flat bodies
like crime scene
victims.
the daddy,
slightly apart
slightly askew.

crooked legs
angled arms
dotted lines
around
the head,
an empty space
where
the heart
should be.

how did they know to preserve Abraham Lincoln's birthplace but destroy mine?

I was born in a thunderstorm,
janitor for a father
mother worked tending bar,
I was named after a family friend
beat to death with a pool stick
the year before I was born.
my first home was a studio
apartment in the back end
of a state line go-go joint
next to the railroad tracks.
my yard was a parking lot
of gravel and broken glass.
the clank and thud of steel
wheels on train track the
soundtrack to my adolescence.

I could have been president
of the United States of America.
it didn't shake out that way.
I became exactly what
the city planners believed
I would become, otherwise,
maybe they wouldn't have
been so quick to destroy
my first home in favor of
an industrial park gartered
with bicycle trails.

it's all gone, now,
the home of my youth.
the bars and clubs and
dope dens, flophouse hotels,
Goldblatt's Department store
consigned to the oblivion
of selective memory.
every building razed to
beautify the corpse of
a city that died with the
shuttering of the steel mills.

upping the irons

by the age of twelve
my bedroom was wall-papered
with Iron Maiden posters.
Eddie in every guise,
my crown jewel being
Live After Death,
Eddie busting out of a grave,
corpse musculature straining,
stringy white hair streaming
away from his skeletal face.
lightning strikes the hinge
securing his skull cap.
the poetic couplet engraved
on the tombstone
introduced me to the
literary cosmic horror
of H.P. Lovecraft.

I remember fondly the
door-sized poster from
Seventh Son of a Seventh Son.
the occult overtones
titillated my young mind
already simmering with
the writings of Aleister Crowley.
the poster illustration depicts
Eddie seated at a desk,
demonic candle burning
to his left, angelic candle

casting light to the right.

I purchased that one
with my paper route money
at the local flea market
along with three Chinese stars
from the ninja gear booth.

every poster was titled:
Phantom of the Opera,
Aces High, Piece of Mind.
Stranger in a Strange Land
with the iconic Eddie
portraying a mash-up of
Blade Runner and
the High Plains Drifter.

these posters and so many
more were procured at the
August Fest, a celebration
of dodgy carnival equipment
and deep-fried junk food,
the highlight of my summer.
every poster was a prize
for busting a balloon with
a dart at a dollar a pop.
Number of the Beast
appealed to this devil-
loving Catholic boy.
Two Minutes to Midnight,
Flight of Icarus,

Somewhere in Time.
Eddie brandishing a cutlass
and a Union Jack as
The Trooper.
Can I Play With Madness?
Powerslave.
all these images supercharged
my hyperactive imagination,
horrified my mother,
perplexed my father.
when my school buddy, Cas,
stopped by to fire up my
newly purchased Nintendo,
he took in my shrine to
this mysterious Iron Maiden
and their monstrous avatar
and asked if I had
any of their albums.

we looked at each other,
blankly, for a moment.

albums?
Iron Maiden's a band?

royal flush

I was ten years old,
seated at the kitchen table
with my mother, father
and grandmother for another
Saturday family poker night.

it was two penny ante
and I played with the
ferocity of a degenerate
gambler playing his last
hand in the no limit
World Series of Poker.

staring blankly at the full
house, fours and sevens,
nestled in my hands,
I was pleasantly surprised
when Gramma raised
three shining pennies.
I met her three cents
and bumped a nickel.
Mom and Dad folded.
Gramma and I escalated
our loose change war
until I blinked
and called her hand.
she laid out her cards,
grinning so wide
her dentures popped out

and landed in her sifter
of peppermint schnapps.

a natural royal flush
in the suit of hearts.

my jaw dropped,
fingers retracting from
the pot as she greedily
swiped the mound of coins
to her bony chest.

I stared at these cards
knowing I'd never again
see this combination.

1 in 650,000 odds.
Gramma won 37 cents.

seed of my destruction

three months shy of
his second birthday,
my son's vocabulary
remains limited to
"drink", "ball", "dog"
and "Cubs lose."

I seem to remember
my daughter at the
same age quoting
Nietzsche and
discussing game theory.

his motor skills are
much further advanced.
he can pitch from a wind-up,
bat balls lobbed to him,
incapacitate a room full
of two-year-olds with
judo chops and front kicks.

my father would have
adored my son's advanced
athleticism but I am
leery of his skills.

I'm well aware the
koan every boy must
kill his father before
becoming a man.

I had my own father
dead a hundred ways
before reaching puberty
before cancer did
what I could not.
it's all metaphorical,
I suppose, but my son
does not deal in
the metaphorical.

not yet two, my son
is already working
on my mortality,
t-ball bats to my knee,
Lego death traps,
jumping on my spleen
while I'm trying to
watch my TV shows.

his eyes burn with a
malevolent intelligence,
yet all he can say is
"Cubs lose. Cubs lose."

trading card killers

I learned early the value
of a Ted Bundy.

I understood the difference
between a Jeffrey Dahmer
and a Son of Sam
or a Boston Strangler.

the cannibals
the spree murderers
the thrill killers

Ed Gein taught me
it's not who you kill
or how many you butcher
as long as you have
a tasteful eye for
interior design.

Henry Lee Lucas
painted life-like fawns
lapping from gentle streams.
John Wayne Gacy
painted silly clowns.
Jack the Ripper
painted the walls of
Whitechapel with whore
blood and blamed it
on the Jews.

Manson configured the
Apocalypse from
a Beatles record.
Ramirez got his
inspiration from
AC/DC's Night Stalker.
Berkowitz claimed
he took his orders from
a neighbor's dog
or a cabal of
devil worshippers
depending on who you ask.

I had them all.
a shoebox full of
trading card killers
stashed with my
porno mags and a
copy of Anton LeVay's
Satanic Bible.

I had them all.
Whitman in the tower.
Starkwether and his gal.
Speck and his nurses.
the entire gamut of
those captured and
those who continue
to elude justice.
the Zodiac.

Green River Killer.
Golden State Killer.

until my mother discovered
my treasure trove
and burned it all
in the fire pit
inexplicably leaving
behind the nylon
cords and the hacksaw.

Halloween

blood
glistens in
the moonlight.

with the
October vibrancy
of
red maple leaves.

Halloween II

a killer cast in flames.
climatic immolation
creating a
cinematic
ginku tree.

searing yellow leaves
licking away
in the
autumn breeze.

Halloween III

for every
season
there is
a mask

a danger
disguised
behind a
thin veneer
of
humanity.

hearts are the
perfect
machine.

a poem for Malachi

there's so much casual cruelty in this world,
and your every nerve ending was attuned
to the mass suffering, the physical misery
and emotional agony wrought upon the
Palestinian people by the callous Israeli
government backed by American lackeys
and their war machine's genocidal capability.

so at protest after protest,
you called for a ceasefire,
an end to Israeli aggression,
an end to Israeli expansion
into the west bank and the
constant harassment of the
civilians living their lives.

but to no avail.

it got to be
there was no more joy to be had
in the creation of experimental music
or solving the daily Wordle,
not when so many innocent
Palestinian men, women and children
were being ruthlessly massacred.

only one obvious option presented itself
and you committed yourself to it
with the single-minded determination

that had defined your character
since first learning war is bad.

after composing your own eulogy
along with an accompanying
glockenspiel solo and posting
them across your social media
platforms and protest websites,
you parked your Volvo along an
off-ramp leading into Nashville.
you mounted a video recorder,
doused yourself in gasoline
raising a Palestinian flag,
flicked a lighter, self-ignited,
creating what you hoped would
become a beacon for the entire world,
a symbol of protest against the
tyranny of the Israeli state
and all those who would seek
to ally themselves with monsters.

but none of the commuters noticed
the vaguely human mobile pyre
and regardless of your ability
to solve puzzles on your phone app
within the first several attempts,
you still underestimated the
searing pain of self-conflagaration.
the flames were so agonizing
you accidentally knocked over
the video recorder and broke

it while you were hopping and
writhing in excruciating torment
of Palestinian proportions.

when your charred husk was
finally discovered, it took
authorities an additional
five days to identify the
reasoning behind the suicide
at which point no one cared.
people do crazy shit every day,
and you got bumped from the news
circuit in favor of a story
involving a serial dog rapist.

however, one can only hope
word of your self-inflicted
martyrdom has managed to
circulate and maybe…
just maybe…
somewhere out there in Gaza
an unfortunate Palestinian child
on the wrong end of an American
made cluster bomb might stop
for a moment before being reduced
to quivering chunks of flesh
and think to oneself
thank you, Malachi.
thank you for everything
you've sacrificed.

blind judgement

despite the money spent on lawyers,
regardless of his family's best hopes,
Alex stared down the probability
of a seven-year prison sentence
for trafficking sixty pounds of weed.

at the hearing, the man queued ahead
was convicted of kidnapping and raping
an eight-year-old child and sentenced
to four years, then gently led away
calm, serene as a pampered politician.

when Alex as called before the judge
and his plea agreement read with its
attendant seven-year term, Alex balked.

"why can't I have four years like that
pedophile you just slapped on the wrist?"

the judge, old and grim as any magistrate
you can imagine, furrowed his brow, said
"well, you can opt for a blind judgement
in which I decide what you'll serve
between four years and twenty years."
Alex's anger became a tiger in the court.
"you're telling me you'd give me
more time for toting a bushel of weed
than that sick fuck molesting kids?

"I'm saying it is a blind judgement.
you will have to take a gamble if
you want to find out how I would rule
against a man trafficking sixty pounds
of marijuana across my state lines."

"you look like a man more forgiving of
a piece of shit raping sixty pounds of kid."

the expensive lawyer chose this moment
to interject himself, counseling Alex
on just how notorious this judge
had proven himself to be on how
hard he ruled against drug crimes.

"sounds like he's hard on kids, too,"
Alex muttered before agreeing to
the plea deal, the seven-year sentence.
the justice system, once again, triumphant.

dream catcher

the biggest surprise
prison held for Alex
was the sheer amount
of white boys
circumstance called
upon him to beat
into the concrete.

crank addicts, mostly.
good ole boys with
mouths like bullhorns
and minds like
wind tunnels.
there seemed to be
something in chronic
methamphetamine
abuse that weakened
their bone density.
one punch to the jaw
would not only
dislodge teeth but
also fracture the bone
along the gum line.

three years in prison
Alex never lost a fight.
having a natural
distaste for white
supremacy, Alex

eschewed his skin
for the First Nation
crew of tribes
within the state
of Oklahoma.
so his penal career
began with the
stomping of certain
Indians who questioned
why a Chicago Polack
should be allowed to
run with the natives.

Cowboy held the keys
to the car at this time.
he immediately found
in Alex a kindred
spirit and welcomed
him into the fold.
going forward, the only
Indians Alex had to
knuckle up were the
new bloods who took
issue with his ancestry.
a quick gladiatorial
meet set up in the
TV room after Dateline,
Alex would deliver an
impersonal beating
followed by a prolonged
and humiliating

face rub into the concrete
cementing another
acceptance that
Alex indeed belonged
to the prison tribe.

from there, it was Nazis
getting pummeled
and the occasional
race riot with the blacks.

he witnessed a man's
lips ripped from his face,
another man, as he held
him down, saw his life
leave his body after
getting his head punted
by an amped-up Cowboy,
the sound sickening
and indescribable and
absolutely unforgettable.

many days brought
many new horrors.
MedFlight choptered
broken bodies out
several times a week
for three years,
but never Alex.
he suffered no
injury more severe

than a few
swollen knuckles.

Alex thrived.
Alex had some laughs.
Alex made friends.
Alex excelled
at arts and crafts,
learned to construct
intricate and beautiful
dream catchers
so exquisite
they eventually
earned Alex his
prison nickname.

fiery bronco

finally home,
back on the wrong side
of Chicago
following three years
busting skulls as
a guest of
Oklahoma State,
Alex desired nothing more
than some time alone
with the closest
approximation of
nature he could find
among the urban blight
and some booze
that didn't taste like
a grape lollipop
dissolved in a vat
of concrete cleaner.

once tearfully reunited
with his '85 Bronco,
he bought a case of
Little King's Ale
and drove fifteen minutes
to the back side
of Wolf Lake
behind Keil Chemical.

twelve beers

and one tire fire
into the night,
Alex became confused,
agitated.
he remembered
filming his Bronco
on his phone's camera,
adoring its simple beauty,
reveling in the joy
of freedom
until it slowly
dawned on him,
probation stipulated
if police intervened
on his good time,
he'd be forced to
serve out the remainder
of his seven year
prison sentence.

paranoia
quickly followed.
fear shattered his
internal compass.
he drove in
every direction as
they became available
going so far as
to follow a set of
railroad tracks until
it improbably dead-ended
at a Chain-link fence.

how is this
even possible?
his mind gibbered.
I grew up here.
how can I be lost?

he sensed
the police closing in.
no lights
no sirens.
circling his position
as silent, invisible
as the Choctaw
he served time with.

his Bronco caught fire
directly thereafter.
he remembered reasoning
he couldn't be arrested
for driving intoxicated
if his Bronco was
torched down to the tires
though he held
no memory of
igniting the inferno.

he liked to believe
maybe the old oil
caking the engine block
finally caught fire.
he loved that Bronco.

the thought of
piloting it again
got him through
many a bad night.

fault or no fault,
it burned down to
its skeletal frame.
police later
picked him up
as he trudged toward
what he hoped was
the direction of his
mother's house and
offered him a ride home.

to this day, he's kept
video on his phone
standing outside
of his mother's house,
his eyes red and engorged
with streaming tears
testifying
maybe the cops ain't so bad
after all.

all my counterfeit kingdoms

boxes of contributor copies
amount to little more than
comfortable abodes for spiders.
bylines fade into bio notes.
the Nerve Cowboys of today
become Wormwood Reviews
two generations removed.
the poetic urge is inexhaustible.
writing the same poem over and
over gets old pretty quick.
chapbooks pile up like discards
in a literary go fish.
the elusive full length
collections land like falling trees
in a forest of the deaf and blind,
yet remains the only proof I have
I did something more than nothing.
all my counterfeit kingdoms
constructed on the shores of
a vast sea of obscurity.

about the author

I first began submitting poetry
to the tiny mimeos back
in late '94, early '95.
Buk was dead and we were
fucking his corpse for all
we were worth.

I was still typing poems
out on a word processor,
a glorified typewriter
with a calculator-sized
screen that allowed me
to edit each page
before I printed it.

three poems to every
submission, every envelope
addressed to a litmag
I found listed in the latest
Poetry Writer's Market.

I wrote more than I read.
I drank more than I wrote.
I worked more than I drank.
I dreamed more than anything.

I wanted to become
a literary superstar,
but the words, the scenes,

the labored metaphors,
all failed to rise
above mediocrity.

but the envelopes kept
being mailed with the
returning acceptances
sprinkled among the
rejection salad like
the occasional olive in
an Olive Garden salad
(see what I mean).

I never had much sense,
but I mustered enough
perseverance to see
a few chapbooks published,
collected a few boxes
of contributor copies,
not one book ever capable
of paying the light bill
or offsetting the price
of a book of stamps.

I watched everything move
to the world wide web.
to emails, blogs, domains,
kudos gathered with
"like" buttons, fame
measured in net traffic,

contributor copies counted
on the amount of Google hits.
now, I read more than write,
write more than drink,
dream of not working.
here, at the end of things,
I wonder at the meaning,
the drive to create
these stories and pieces
of free verse narratives
I'm compelled to share
with the mostly apathetic.

everything is forgotten
the moment I write it,
the second you read it.
libraries crammed with
an abundance of words,
bookstores can't give it
away fast enough.

I'm lighting my own match
amidst an inferno
and describing my smoke
to everyone burning.

in the end, I suppose
I amused myself.
that's the best I can say
about any endeavor
I've turned my mind toward.

it was more fulfilling
than watching sitcoms.
it engaged me more
than any episode of
whatever bullshit talent
show any bullshit network
had to offer.
it was all I had to offer;
these cinders I leave behind.

Karl Koweski is a displaced Region Rat now living in rural Alabama. He writes when his pen allows it. He's a husband to a lovely wife and father to some fantastic kids. He collects pop culture ephemera. On most days he prefers Flash Gordon to Luke Skywalker and Neil Diamond to Elvis Presley.

MORE ROADSIDE PRESS TITLES:

By Plane, Train or Coincidence
Michele McDannold

Prying
Jack Micheline, Charles Bukowski and Catfish McDaris

Wolf Whistles Behind the Dumpster
Dan Provost

*Busking Blues: Recollections of a Chicago Street Musician
and Squatter*
Westley Heine

Unknowable Things
Kerry Trautman

How to Play House
Heather Dorn

Kiss the Heathens
Ryan Quinn Flanagan

St. James Infirmary
Steven Meloan

Street Corner Spirits
Westley Heine

A Room Above a Convenience Store
William Taylor Jr.

Resurrection Song
George Wallace

Nothing and Too Much to Talk About
Nancy Patrice Davenport

MORE ROADSIDE PRESS TITLES:

MORE ROADSIDE PRESS TITLES:

Disposable Darlings
Todd Cirillo

Full Moon Midnight
Belinda Subraman

Innocent Postcards
John Pietaro

Cistern Latitudes
James Duncan

Another Saturday Night in Jukebox Hell
Alan Catlin